# ICELAND

*Wild at Heart*

*ICELAND – Wild at Heart*


JPV útgáfa · Reykjavík · 2017

Layout and cover design: Jón Ásgeir
Main font: Bernhard Modern BT 10.5/14 pt
Printing: Prentmiðlun / Latvia

*Published in Reykjavík, a UNESCO City of Literature*



ISBN 978-9935-11-774-8

JPV útgáfa is an imprint of Forlagið ehf.
www.forlagid.is

# ICELAND

## *Wild at Heart*

EINAR GUÐMANN &
GYÐA HENNINGSDÓTTIR

JPV ÚTGÁFA

# Contents

# VISIONS OF ICELAND

In the distance Hælavíkurbjarg looms out of the darkness as drifting snow accentuates the wintry world of Hornstrandir. The chronicles tell us that in 1321 a polar bear came ashore at Hælavík and killed eight people, "tore them all apart and ate some of them". Stories like this are indicative of the struggle faced by those who have tried to survive in this harsh environment.

What comes to mind when we think about Iceland? What makes it special? As photographers, we would say the light, the glaciers, the volcanic activity, the highlands, the spectacular coastline and the contrasts between summer and winter. The birds and wildlife also have a big part to play. We live in the far north where life is a struggle for survival and both men and beasts are at the mercy of nature's whims. The chapters in this book reflect our own experiences of the things that we feel define our homeland.

Most of the photographs in the book are free from human constructions and other signs of human activity. When footpaths and viewing platforms are visible, the experience of untouched nature is invalidated. We attempt to show the things that we believe make Iceland special in the hope of raising the value of untouched nature in the mind of the reader. In a world ruled by economic interests where we tend to prioritise short-term profit over the protection of nature, untouched nature does not stand much of a chance if ignored by the authorities. The conservation of habitats for certain species and the preservation of unspoiled landscapes are becoming ever more important, but also more difficult.

It is a privilege to have the opportunity to spend years travelling around Iceland taking photographs. Photography is not just our way of experiencing and getting closer to nature and natural forces. A moment of beauty in nature touches the soul. It evokes a feeling of love and compassion for something precious, which hopefully raises awareness of the importance of preserving untouched nature. As the Icelandic proverb says, "better unscathed than well healed".

# POWER

Holuhraun became global news in 2014 when one of the largest lava eruptions in history began. It is believed that an eruption took place at the same site around 1800. The lava field is far from any inhabited area.

Following the Laki eruptions of 1783–84, famine hit Iceland. Acid rain following the ash fall from the Laki craters burnt holes in leaves and singed the skins of men and beasts. A haze hung in the atmosphere and 60% of all livestock in Iceland died within a year. In the "Haze Famine" that followed, more than 20% of the population died from hunger or other hardship. This is just one of the many volcanic eruptions that have made their mark on Icelandic history. A nation that regularly experiences natural disasters in the wake of volcanic activity develops respect for the power of the earth.

Iceland is on a hotspot, where a mantle plume from the bowels of the earth transports magma to the surface. Decades may pass between volcanic eruptions, but really the country is young in terms of geological time. Iceland rests on the boundary where the North American and Eurasian tectonic plates meet, which is an area of intense volcanic activity. A volcanic eruption is not an entertaining natural spectacle but a terrible force that has threatened the nation throughout history, causing suffering and death through ash fall and flooding that have led to famine.

When you set foot on recently cooled lava, you make a sound like walking on broken glass. It is an unforgettable experience. In our travels through Iceland we always keep in mind the danger that the power of the earth represents. Awe, humility and just a touch of fear strike you as you walk over uneven lava where an eruption took place. Steam winds its way up into the cold air, reminding us of what lurks below. The terror of an unknown force underfoot hangs in the air. We are reminded of this power in the bowels of the earth every day in our travels around Iceland. Boiling hot springs, gargantuan volcanoes, craters and hot pools remind us of the danger. Remind us of our history.

There have been just over 200 volcanic eruptions in Iceland since the settlement. On average, there are 20–25 eruptions per century, and in any given decade there may be anywhere from zero to 10–12 eruptions.

Iceland lies on the boundary between the North American and Eurasian tectonic plates, which are diverging. This boundary is an area of high volcanic activity. In the early days of the eruption at Holuhraun, the earth could be seen splitting apart as the lava found its way to the surface.

Holuhraun was one of the largest eruptions of recent times. The surface area of the resulting lava field is around 85 $km^2$, with a thickness of around 16 m.

The eruption at Holuhraun lasted six months. Since the systematic recording of volcanic eruptions began, there has been an eruption in Iceland every three to five years on average. Some eruptions die down within a few hours, while others last for weeks or months on end.

The moon peeps through a plume of ash at Holuhraun.
Toxic fumes and gases made any approach to the eruption site hazardous, so it was best to stay upwind.

Clouds of vapour rise into the sky as the glowing lava
flows into the river Jökulsá á Fjöllum. In the darkness, it was hard
to distinguish between the lava and the water.

The hot spring Fagrihver at Hveravellir
resembles a blue eye surrounded by the shelves of
silica deposits that give it its striking beauty.

Hverarönd, to the east of Námafjall, is one of the largest mudpot sites in Iceland. There are a large number of mudpots in a dazzling array of colours resulting from sulphur deposits.

Boiling water and steam spew violently from two openings in Öskurhóll, the most renowned volcanic spring at Hveravellir. The oldest description of the site dates from 1752, when it got its name (which translates to Roaring Mound) because of the fearsome roaring and whistling sounds it emitted.

The Hveraröndur area near Námafjall is a popular tourist destination. A long time ago, sulphur was mined here and exported, making a fortune for the landowners. Today the value of the land lies first and foremost in its power to attract tourists.

Light brown rhyolite is a distinguishing feature of Kerlingarfjöll, but the peripheral mountains are formed from tuff. Icelandic folklore tells of outlaws and evil spirits in the Kerlingarfjöll mountains, which doubtless goes some way to explaining why sheep were not herded there until after the middle of the 19th century.

Kerlingarfjöll is a beautiful cluster of mountains to the southwest of the glacier Hofsjökull. It is an area of intense geothermal activity, most concentrated in the Hveradalir valleys.

Coming to Askja and standing on the brink of the crater Víti, separated from Öskjuvatn lake by a thin wall, is an unforgettable experience. Víti is believed to have formed in a explosion during the eruption of Askja on 29 March 1875. In such a magnificent landscape, we get a sense of how small we really are.

# THE LIGHT

Vatnaöldur is a series of tephra craters near the Veiðivötn lakes. There was an eruption here around the time of the settlement. The resulting layer of tephra is called the settlement layer and has often been useful for dating archaeological remains.

We are in a never-ending race with the light. A landscape photographer cannot expect to get much sleep over the summer months if the intention is to photograph both sunset and sunrise. Most foreign photographers who visit Iceland are struck first by the light. The soft and constantly changing light is a distinctive feature of our country. At sunrise and sunset, the light takes on hues that, in their diversity, can always surprise you. It is mesmerising, and undeniably a privilege, to witness such a spectacle. Photographers wait patiently for the light. We hike up mountains and wait for what may come. No two sunsets are the same.

In every sunrise and every sunset comes that moment when the vibrancy of the light reaches its zenith. Heaven and earth are infused with colour as the first or last rays of the sun bathe everything in golden light. This is the moment we try to capture on camera. This is the reason photographers do not sleep in the summer.

Iceland has countless treasures to offer the photographer as the light swings between the extremes of summer and winter. On the summer solstice, 20–22 June, the sun merely grazes the horizon for a few moments before rising again in a true festival of colour, weather and cloud cover permitting. In the darkest months of winter, however, it often never truly becomes light. Daylight lasts just a few short hours and every ray from the sun is a precious gift. Some days never seem to get bright. Shades of grey blanket everything. After a long, dark winter, every glimpse of the sun is a welcome sight. This is the reason that we Icelandic photographers value the light so highly; it is one of the most special things about the country.

Svartifoss waterfall is in Skaftafell National Park. Towering basalt columns make the site particularly beautiful. It is believed that Guðjón Samúelsson, the architect behind Hallgrímskirkja Church, was inspired by the waterfall.

Kirkjufell on the Snæfellsnes peninsula is one of the most popular spots for photographers in Iceland. The mountain, which is 463 m high, is located near the town of Grundarfjörður. In the foreground is Kirkjufellsfoss.

The northern lights are reflected in the sea
by the rock arch Gatanöf, just north of Húsavík.

Látrabjarg is the westernmost point of Iceland. It is home to millions of birds, the largest seabird colony in Iceland, including the tamest puffins in the country. The cliff has been the final resting place for a lot of people. Many ships have been wrecked at the bottom of the cliff, with no survivors. Before 1925 people abseiled down the cliff in search of eggs and birds. That year 14,000 birds and 40,000 eggs were taken, but the next year two young men died, and the practice was discontinued.

Goðafoss in Bárðardalur is one of the most beautiful waterfalls in Iceland. The waterfall gets its name, which means Waterfall of the Gods, from a story about Þorgeir, the chieftain of Ljósavatn. It is said that he threw his pagan idols into the falls after converting to Christianity.

At the sight of the Aurora Borealis dancing in Þingvallavatn, the heart fills with joy and a childlike wonder at this colourful and mysterious phenomenon. The Aurora Borealis is named after Aurora, the Roman goddess of the dawn.

Landmannalaugar is one of the most popular tourist destinations in the Icelandic wilderness. The rhyolite in the mountains gives them their colour and beauty and there are few places in Iceland that can rival the dazzling vibrancy of this landscape.

Nauthúsagil is a long, narrow ravine near the track into Þórsmörk. The river Nauthúsaá flows through the ravine.

Seljalandsfoss is one of the tallest and most spectacular waterfalls in Iceland. Visitors can walk behind the waterfall.

The surf batters Malarrif in the foreground, and as the sun rises the Lóndrangar sea stacks and the ancient volcano Snæfellsjökull are at their most beautiful. The two stacks, 61 and 75 m high, are volcanic plugs from an old volcanic crater. In times gone by, eagles nested on the taller of the stacks. Snæfellsjökull itself has long been shrouded in mystery, not least thanks to the novel *Journey to the Centre of the Earth* by Jules Verne, in which the protagonist's journey begins by descending into the volcano.

To the east of Mývatn lake stands the 2,500-year-old volcanic crater Hverfjall, around 140 m deep and 1,000 m in diameter. The crater was formed in a Plinian eruption and is believed to be one of the largest craters of its kind in the world. In the centre of the crater is a mound around 20 m high.

The river Kverná flows into a ravine east of Ytri-Skógar. The site is particularly impressive as visitors can walk behind the waterfall as it cascades down into the ravine.

Sand dunes in the vast expanse east of Herðubreið form a multilayered spectacle in the evening sun. Areas of untouched wilderness in Iceland have decreased by around 68% since 1936. If this trend continues, by 2032 there will be no untouched wilderness left in Iceland.

Borgin on Grímsey is a formation of basalt columns that appears at its most beautiful as the evening sun peeps across from the north. Traditionally, the rock was believed to be a church for the elves on Grímsey.

# GLACIERS AND ICE

A glaucous gull dances on an ice floe in the glacial lagoon Jökulsárlón. A wet ice floe forms a blue background.

Iceland is set apart by its glaciers. It is believed that around 9,000 years ago there were no glaciers in Iceland, and that until 2,500 years ago the climate was mild. Then the planet started to cool and glaciers began to form. They probably peaked around 1900, but have been shrinking and retreating since then. Today around 11% of the surface of Iceland is covered by glaciers and Vatnajökull, the largest glacier in Europe, grows smaller and thinner each year.

Glaciers are simply water in solid form. They are the largest reservoirs of fresh water on the planet. All the largest water courses in Iceland originate in the glaciers, the source of around a third of all the water that flows into the sea each year. Glaciers are formed when more snow falls than melts for many years in a row. With the right conditions, the snow turns to glacial ice in five to six years.

In the history of Iceland, glaciers are more often than not linked to disaster. Many of them cover volcanoes that have been active over the centuries, such as Grímsvötn and Bárðarbunga. Volcanic eruptions under glaciers can have catastrophic consequences, since they often cause flooding that destroys everything in its path. It is an incredible experience to walk on a glacier and look upon the glacier caves that form within them. However, it is also a hazardous environment that must be treated with respect and a little healthy fear. The glaciers are an inextricable part of Icelandic nature and one of the most distinctive features of the country. Photographing glacier caves and walking on glaciers is not without danger and it is safest to restrict such activity to the warmer months. Glaciers and ice are integral features of Icelandic nature and, in their own way, define the country and the national character.

Enormous ice floes regularly wash up on the lower shore of Jökulsárlón. The blue colour of the ice is due to the fact that snow falling on a glacier is compacted over time. Air bubbles are squeezed out, the ice becomes more dense and as it reaches a certain volume, the blue colour is amplified. Water absorbs blue light to a lesser degree than other colours in the spectrum, which is why deep lakes appear to have a blueish hue.

Below the glacier Fjallsjökull is Fjallsárlón. The lagoon lies just to the west of Jökulsárlón. The river Fjallsá flows out of the lagoon down to the sea at Breiðárlón.

An Arctic tern feeds a sand eel to its chick. The chick begins to call shortly before the parent lands with the food – the amazing thing is that the chick appears to recognise its parents from a distance among the multitude flocking above.

Jökulsárlón lies at the foot of the glacier Breiðamerkurjökull, one of the most popular tourist destinations in Iceland. Jökulsárlón is the deepest lake in Iceland at a depth of 248 m.

Kvíárjökull is an outlet glacier extending from Öræfajökull down a 500–600 m deep gorge between Staðarfjall and Vatnafjöll. Around 2,500 years ago, the glacier was much larger and created huge crests, Kvíamýrarkambur to the west and Kambsmýrarkambur to the east.

The surface of Kötlujökull is rough and jagged where its slopes begin to drop down. The glacier is 300–400 m thick. Katla itself is located on the southwest side of Mýrdalsjökull and is one of the most notorious volcanoes in Iceland. Katla last erupted in 1918.

Skaftafellsjökull is one of the outlet glaciers extending from Vatnajökull, east of Skaftafellsheiði. Due to climate change, glaciers in Iceland are retreating rapidly. They give way to sand and gravel, and after many years vegetation begins to take root, as we can see at Skaftafellsjökull.

Glacier caves, such as this one in the vicinity of Landmannalaugar, are a captivating but treacherous phenomenon. Glacier caves are formed under certain conditions, in particular when running water erodes a channel through the snow and ice.

Jökulsárlón is one of the most photographed locations in Iceland.
The glacier and lagoon are in constant flux with the tides and a never-ending supply of new ice from the glacier. The lagoon teems with wildlife.

Jökulsárlón is a source of food for a large number of bird species and seals. At high tide, fish and sand eels are washed into the lagoon, providing food for Arctic terns, kittiwakes and skuas. When they aren't fishing, the birds rest on the ice floes slowly drifting down the lagoon.

# WATER

Lómagnúpur once jutted into the sea and is one of the highest promontories in Iceland. In *Njáls saga* Flosi Þórðarson dreams on Svínafell that a giant comes out of the mountain, dressed in goatskins and carrying an iron staff. This giant is today one of the four guardians of Iceland, as featured in the Icelandic coat of arms, protecting the south coast from the forces of evil.

The value of waterfalls and water channels was once measured in kilowatt-hours. Today, their worth is no less measured in hours of wonder. Waterfalls and lakes are a huge part of Icelandic nature and their significant role in attracting tourists to Iceland makes them economically important. In his time, the geologist Dr Sigurður Þórarinsson penned an essay in which he implored the nation to remember that in Iceland's waterfalls lies a value that cannot be measured in money, but in wonder. Little did he know that the wonder of tourists would one day form the bedrock of the economy. In a similar vein, the poet Einar Benediktsson once imagined selling the northern lights. Everyone knows that this is possible. You just have to look at the number of northern lights tours on offer in Iceland today.

Waterfalls and lakes are probably the features most photographed by those who travel the country. Watching a beautiful waterfall is mesmerising. It is not only about seeing but about the full sensual experience. The vibration, the thunder, the sheer volume. Lakes in Iceland have various origins. Some were formed by glacial erosion in the Ice

Age, such as Skorradalsvatn and Lagarfljót, and today the warming climate swells the glacial lagoons as the glaciers retreat. Volcanic activity formed Ljósavatn and Hreðavatn, while land subsistence and tectonic deformations are behind Þingvallavatn and Skjálftavatn. Hraunsvatn in Öxnadalur was formed by landslides. Lakes therefore have different creation stories. Water is a valuable resource, at once for drinking, generating kilowatts and as a source of wonder. A waterfall cascading over a mountain ledge is a visual resource, attracting photographers and tourists from all over the world.

It is possible to walk behind Seljalandsfoss, although visitors must tread carefully as the constant spray makes the path slippery. Standing behind the waterfall is an incredible experience.

Skógafoss is one of Iceland's most magnificent waterfalls.
It is 60 m high, cascading over ancient sea cliffs. Legend has it that Þrasi,
a settler in Skógar, hid a chest of gold in a cave behind the falls.

At the head of the valley Þjórsárdalur lies the waterfall Granni. The Fossá river splits into two channels, creating two waterfalls: Háifoss and its neighbour Granni.

Fosså in Fossárdalur flows into Háifoss, which at 122 m
is one of the highest waterfalls in Iceland. Like its neighbour Granni,
Háifoss lies at the head of Þjórsárdalur.

One of the waterfalls in the river Kirkjufellsá.

Eystrahorn is a majestic mountain above the farm of Hvalnes. The mountain is primarily composed of gabbro and granophyre, so-called plutonic rocks which formed as magma solidified deep inside the earth. The rock has been found to contain gold, silver, mercury and other metals.

Altogether there are six waterfalls in the river Dynjandisá and the entire area is truly a feast for the eyes. Today, Dynjandi is one of the most popular tourist attractions in the West Fjords.

Dynjandi has sometimes mistakenly been called Fjallfoss. It is difficult to comprehend the size of the waterfall, which lies at the head of Arnarfjörður fjord, without walking right up to it and hearing the din from which it gets its name. It is 30 m wide at the top and 60 m wide at the bottom.

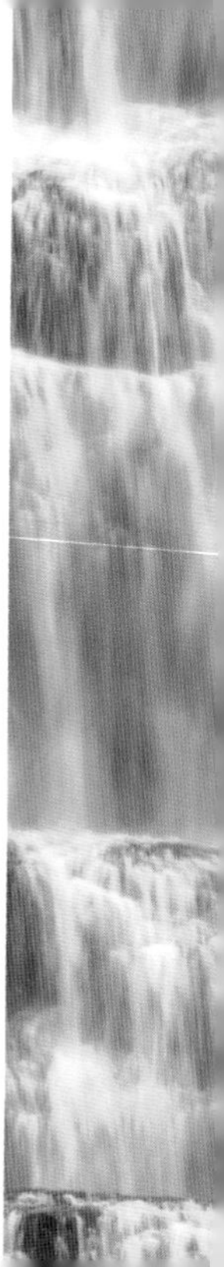

Öxarárfoss, one of the jewels of Þingvellir, is notable for the fact that it is man-made. It seems likely that the medieval Icelanders wanted to provide water for those attending the Althing national assembly, as well as adding to the beauty of the assembly site. It is possible that the ancient belief in nature spirits also had a part to play, since gods and wights were thought to dwell in waterfalls and so Öxarárfoss would attract their powers to Þingvellir.

Litlanesfoss falls into the river Hengifossá in Fljótsdalur.
It cascades over rock surrounded by spectacular basalt columns and indeed is sometimes called Stuðlafoss, meaning Column Falls.
The basalt columns are unusually tall and straight.

Gljúfrabúi falls from Gljúfurá river into a ravine, which visitors may walk through, although not without getting wet. An enchanting light filters down into the ravine and the area is rich with greenery.

Brúarfoss falls into a narrow rift. The interplay of water and rock is an impressive spectacle. Jón Gerreksson, the bishop of Skálholt, met his end here. The story has it that he was a "scoundrel" and when the farmers were fed up of his mischief, he was stuffed into a sack and drowned in the Brúará river on 20 July 1433.

Dettifoss in the river Jökulsá á Fjöllum is the most powerful waterfall in Europe. The astonishing power, noise and sheer volume of water at Dettifoss is hard to convey with a photograph. It is well worth sitting a while near the waterfall to contemplate its incredible force.

Dettifoss can be viewed from both the east and west banks.
Below, the falls give way to the ravine Jökulsárgljúfur. It is believed that the ravine was formed extremely rapidly in an enormous flood when a dam containing a glacial lake burst and the lake drained in a matter of hours.

Brúarfoss is a distinctive waterfall near a group of summerhouses at Brekkuskógur. Until 1602 there was a traversable stone arch over the Brúará river. It is said that the steward at Skálholt was behind the destruction of the arch, as he and the Bishop's wife were horrified at the encroachment of vagrants, who flocked to Skálholt in times of famine.

Þorgeir was the chieftain of Ljósavatn. In 1000 AD, he retreated under a fur cloak at the Althing national assembly to choose between Christianity and Norse paganism. He represented the pagans but nevertheless declared that all Icelanders should convert to Christianity, although idol worship, the exposure of infants and the consumption of horse meat would continue to be legal if conducted in secret. When Þorgeir returned home from the Althing, it is said that he cast his idols into Goðafoss.

Folaldafoss in the river Berufjarðará lies a short distance from the ancient mountain pass over Öxi, easily reached from the road. The perfect spot to stop for a picnic. In the distance the head of the fjord Berufjörður can be seen.

Water flows from under an area of Hallmundarhraun lava field into the Hvítá river. The waterfall Hraunfossar is surrounded by vegetation and the autumn brightness accentuates the interplay of water, light and colour.

Þingvellir has a special place in Icelandic history, as well as being designated a UNESCO World Heritage Site. The Althing national assembly was established there in 930 and convened annually until 1798. This was the site at which Þorgeir, chieftain of Ljósavatn, declared Iceland to be a Christian nation, and also the site at which Icelanders declared independence on 17 June 1944. Evidence of the earth's crust pulling apart is everywhere at Þingvellir – Iceland straddles the divergent boundary between two tectonic plates.

# THE HIGHLANDS

Hattafell is on the Fjallabak route. In the foreground is Svartikrókur and the canyon Markarfljótsgljúfur.

Ever since the settlement, people in Iceland have chosen to live by the coast. The main arteries of the country run through the lowlands. In contrast, there are the vast expanses of the highlands. There biting winds howl across glaciers and plains, the forces of nature are hostile and the weather can turn in an instant. In times gone by, people travelled over the highlands when they needed to get across the country, even in the autumn and winter months. Such journeys often meant death for those who ventured on them and many stories have been told of unlucky travellers, such as the brothers from Reynisstaðir who died of exposure on Kjölur in the autumn of 1780. They disappeared into the dark with their horses and sheep. People stopped traversing the highlands for a century afterwards, since they took such a toll on the nation.

Travel in the highlands has increased more recently. No one could be left unmoved by the highlands in all their glorious diversity: Landmannalaugar, Askja, Kverkfjöll, Kerlingarfjöll or Sprengisandur. The beating heart of the highlands, though, is impossible to capture in a picture. It lies in the limitless expanses, the colours of the mountains, the tranquillity, pausing to listen to the silence, broken only by the creaking of the glaciers. Sensing the vastness and the unending plains of the wilderness.

The central highlands of Iceland are the largest area in Europe completely unsettled by humans. It is somewhat paradoxical that this is the feature that attracts people, and yet increased access through tourism and road construction is its biggest threat. Hopefully there will always be areas and paths in Iceland free from the hustle and bustle of people. The fates of our forebears remind us that the highlands deserve our respect.

Mælifell is a tuff peak standing on the plain between the glaciers Torfajökull and Mýrdalsjökull. The Fjallabak route traverses the plain, known as Mælifellssandur.

The Landmannalaugar area is 600 m above sea level. It is the most significant location in Iceland for rhyolite and high-temperature geothermal activity.
The landscape is colourful and unique, unrivalled in the variety of rhyolite formations and resulting hues. Some of the mountains were formed under a glacier, but some of the colours resulted from the effects of high temperatures and acid on the rock.

A short distance from Landmannalaugar lies Bláhylur, a stunning blue lake in a crater believed to have formed 1130 years ago in a Plinian eruption. It also goes by the names Hnausapollur and Tjörvafellspollur, but in ancient times was known as Litlavíti (Little Hell).

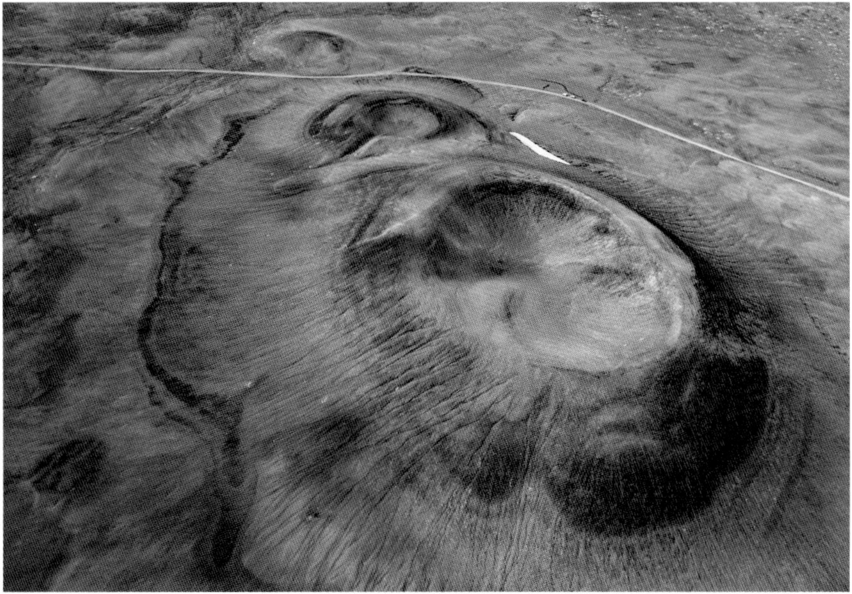

Craters in the sands a short distance from Bláhylur and the southern Fjallabak route. If you look carefully, you may spot the tourists who drove their cars off-road, erasing their tracks under the supervision of a ranger.

Landmannalaugar is widely considered to be the heart of the Icelandic highlands, in the middle of the Fjallabak Nature Reserve east of Hekla. The natural beauty and colourful rocks that define the area make it ideal for camping and hiking expeditions.

Moss and sulphur colour the slopes of Brenni-steinsalda, a short distance from Landmanna-laugar. The area is full of geothermal activity – a fissure vent in the Lauga-hraun lava field splits the mountain.

Bláhnúkur is one of the most popular mountains in Landmannalaugar. Trails from all directions lead to the mountain and the view from the summit is breathtaking.

Herðubreið in the Ódáðahraun lava field is often called "the queen of Icelandic mountains". It is a 1,682 m tuff mountain formed when a volcano erupted under a glacier. Lava right at the peak tells us that the eruption broke through the glacier. Herðubreið was once voted the national mountain of Iceland.

The view east from Bláhnúkur is spectacular. It has been theorised that the area around Torfajökull glacier bears the characteristics of a major volcanic site in its dying days. Volcanic and geothermal activity in the area indicates the formation of a caldera, the rim of which would be defined by Barmur, Suðurnámur and Háalda.

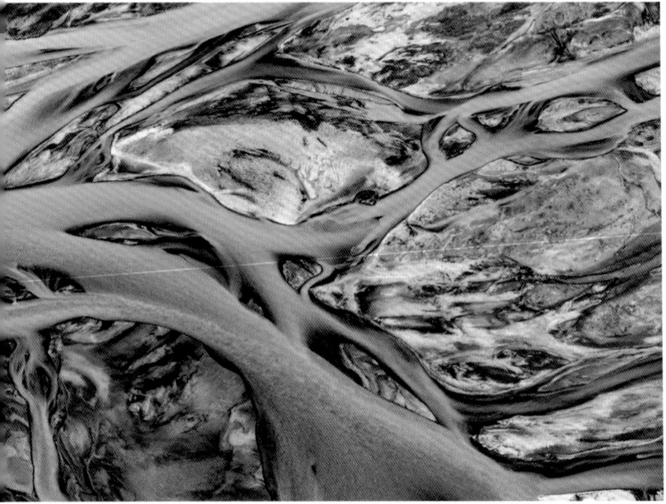

The colour of the riverbed in Tungnaá near lake Blautaver, a short distance from Veiðivötn, reflects the geology of the area. Tungnaá has been dammed for hydroelectric power at Búrfell, Vatnsfell, Hrauneyjafoss and Sultartangi, before finally flowing into the river Þjórsá.

In many places, the colours of the Kerlingarfjöll mountains are similar to Landmanna-laugar. The rocks contain obsidian.It is believed that the mountains were formed in the later part of the Ice Age.

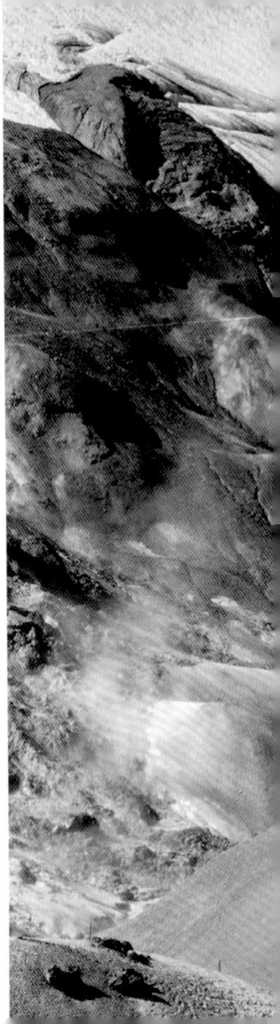

Stórkonufell, lush with greenery, towers over the plains, as seen from the Emstra route. This photograph was taken from Entujökull, one of the outlet glaciers of Mýrdalsjökull. In the foreground is the river Fremri-Emstruá, while the background features the mountains Stóra-Mófell, Mófells-hnausar, Litla-Mófell and Stórkonufell.

# THE WILDLIFE

Efforts to eradicate the Arctic fox with poison almost led to the eradication of the white-tailed eagle in Iceland in the first half of the nineteenth century. The population has never recovered. Measures to protect the species enacted since 1970 have been slow to pay dividends, since there are only around 30 breeding pairs each year and so the number of chicks surviving their first winter is low. White-tailed eagles are tremendously sensitive to interferences at the nest site and prefer to nest a long way from any human activity.

Icelandic wildlife is characterised by the country's remoteness and climate. Only six species of wild land mammals can be found in Iceland, as well as two species of seals that pup here. These are the Arctic fox, the mink, the reindeer, the brown rat, the field mouse and the house mouse. That is all. The Arctic fox is the only land mammal that reached Iceland without the help of humans. Mink were imported to Iceland in 1931 to be farmed for their fur, which proved to be a disaster for Icelandic nature. Reindeer were imported in the seventeenth century and have roamed wild ever since. Polar bears have found their way to Iceland, but since they rely on sea ice, they have never settled here. Rats and mice accompanied the settlers around 1,100 years ago. The oldest legal code in Iceland, the Grey Goose Laws, states that it is forbidden to bring red foxes, wolves or brown bears into the country, with harsh punishments for anybody doing so. (Brown bears and wolves would have found it difficult to get a foothold, but the red fox would have been able to settle in Iceland and would then undoubtedly have eradicated the Arctic fox, as it did in neighbouring countries.)

The birdlife of Iceland is characterised by a low number of species and high degree of specialisation. Only 75 species regularly nest here in Iceland, although over 100 species have been known to do so at least once. Sea and wetland species are in the overwhelming majority (80%), with few species preferring dry land (20%). Only three species of raptors regularly nest here: the gyrfalcon, the white-tailed eagle and the merlin. The short-eared owl is the only owl to nest in Iceland, although snowy owls are occasionally sighted and used to nest here.

In the mating season for Arctic foxes, the vixen is in charge and the male fox follows her wherever she goes. Shyness around photographers is momentarily forgotten as the foxes concentrate on the important matter of preserving the species. In neighbouring countries, the fertility of Arctic foxes is determined by the availability of food, but this has not been shown to be the case in Iceland. Icelandic vixens bear young every year. Year-round fox hunting is believed to be the reason that there is always territory to spare for young and inexperienced animals.

The Arctic fox population was large around the middle of the twentieth century but is now in decline, and it is believed that by the end of the 70s there were only 1,000 foxes in Iceland. Climate change led to increased numbers of birds, an important food source for Arctic foxes, especially fulmars, pink-footed geese and golden plovers, and so the fox population rose. Growing bird populations and mild winters have therefore played a part in increasing fox numbers.

Reindeer were imported to Iceland around the end of the eighteenth century with the aim of farming them, as the Sami have done since ancient times. This was not successful and so reindeer have always roamed wild in Iceland. The reindeer population is around 7,000 in the summer. Sustainable hunting takes place.

Eaglets are highly vulnerable in their first weeks, dependent on their parents for shelter from the elements. A large proportion of their diet comes from the sea, but white-tailed eagles will seek food wherever they can. Eaglets take a long time to reach self-sufficiency and many do not survive their first winter. On 10 November 1913, the Icelandic parliament passed a law to protect white-tailed eagles. However, it was not until the poisoning of Arctic foxes was banned in 1964 that the eagle population slowly began to recover – today there are only around 30 breeding pairs each year.

A total of 390 different bird species have been spotted in Iceland, out of the 10,500 species known in the world, but only 75 species nest here. The horned grebe is primarily a migrant and the only species of the grebe family to nest in Iceland. Its preferred habitat is the lushly vegetated ponds of the lowlands, with their plentiful supplies of sticklebacks and aquatic insects. It is a species that struggles to adapt to changes in its environment. The draining of the wetlands through ditch digging between 1945 and 1970 has been the biggest disruption of habitat in the history of Iceland, destroying important areas for birdlife. Some of these areas have been restored, creating a brighter future for the horned grebe and other bird species.

Iceland is home to many of the largest seabird populations in Europe. The guillemot is a common species in Iceland and is one of the seabirds believed to be vulnerable to environmental changes in the oceans as the climate warms. The guillemot is a cliff-nesting bird that does not require a large nesting site. Seventy guillemots have been known to nest in just one square metre of cliff. The guillemot claims a tiny spot on the cliff and lays a single egg. Once the egg is laid, the parents work as a team to protect it and raise the chick. In an international context, Iceland plays a key role for many bird species, not least the seabird populations.

The Barrow's goldeneye duck is much admired by bird lovers. North East Iceland is the most popular breeding area in Europe for these ducks, with Lake Mývatn the preferred location. It is drawn by the nutrient-rich waters and prefers to nest in holes and hollows. Since it is such a creature of habit, it is not thought likely that the Barrow's goldeneye will spread to other areas of Iceland and therefore it is extremely important that its habitat is protected.

Mink were originally imported to Iceland in 1931 to be farmed for their fur,
but this proved to be an ill-fated venture. The animals very soon escaped from their
cages and were quick to breed and adapt to the Icelandic environment.
It took around 40 years for the population to spread across the entire country.

The Icelandic ptarmigan is believed to have originated in Greenland. It is one of the major game species in Iceland, commonly served at Christmas. Its population is extremely prone to fluctuation, but it is a very fertile species.

The gyrfalcon holds an important place in the national imagination of Icelanders and was once included in the country's coat of arms. It also features strongly in medieval Icelandic literature and Norse mythology. The ptarmigan is an important food source for the gyrfalcon, of which there are only 300–400 breeding pairs in Iceland.

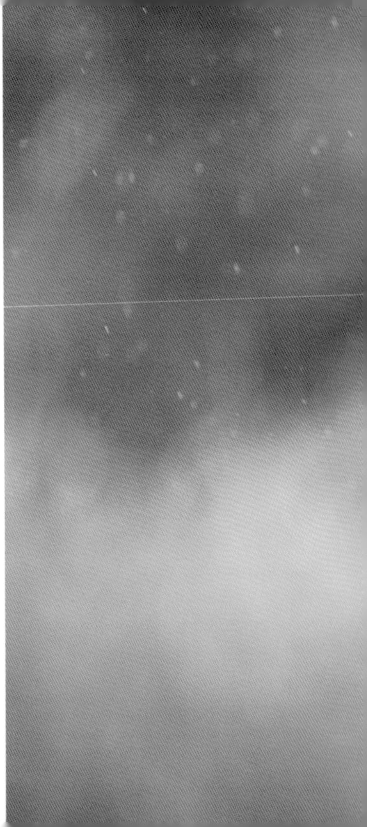

A skua, a glaucous gull and a kittiwake fight over a morsel of food at Jökulsárlón. The kittiwake will not hesitate to dive beneath the surface, but the skua avoids the water, instead using its spectacular aerial agility to rob other birds.

There are believed to be around 3 million pairs of puffins in Iceland. Its colourful Roman nose is its most distinctive feature and can carry a large number of sand eels in one trip. The puffin is a skilled diver, appearing to fly beneath the surface – it can reach depths of up to 70 m. It is, however, rather clumsy in the air, endowed with small wings better suited to diving than flying.

The great northern diver is a stunning bird that defends its territory with a wailing and yodelling sound. When courting, the great northern diver puts on an impressive show, dancing with rhythmic and synchronised movements. This behaviour is probably intended to impress the mate and demonstrate superiority. Despite the beauty of this majestic bird, there are a number of negative words in Icelandic referencing the great northern diver, with definitions such as 'rogue' and 'complaining'.

Around three weeks before laying her eggs, the female gyrfalcon stops hunting, takes up residence in the nest and waits for the male to bring her food. If he performs well, she will lay her eggs. When the chicks are two to three weeks old, the female begins to hunt again. Gyrfalcons mate for life.

The bearded seal is a rare visitor to Iceland. It subsists mainly on crabs, shrimps and shellfish and prefers to live on broken sea ice.

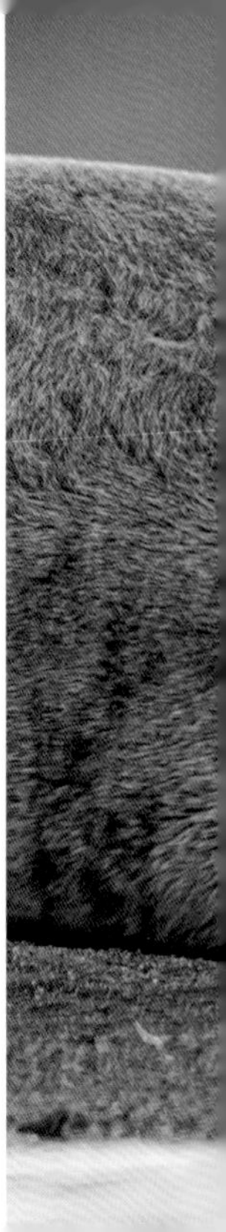

A colourful puffin resting as the sun sets at Látrabjarg. Puffins nest all over Iceland, but the largest colonies are found in the Westman Islands, Grímsey and Látrabjarg.

An Arctic tern hunting in Hólstjörn pond on Grímsey. The Arctic tern undertakes the longest migration of all birds. It flies around 40,000 km a year, which is the equivalent of flying all the way around the world. It is a long-lived bird that may reach the age of 30 and is very much a creature of habit, preferring to nest on the same tussock year after year. It is therefore vulnerable to disruptions to its habitat.

Humpback whales are very common around Iceland in the summer months, when they head north in search of food. It is not known why humpback whales leap out of the water like this one in Skjálfandaflói bay near Húsavík, although scientists have suggested several theories. One theory is that it is a form of communication, another that they are trying to rid themselves of parasites and a third that they are simply having fun.

The view of the mountains from the sea is stunning, while in the foreground we can see a humpback whale searching for food in the waters west of Grímsey. There are a lot of whales to be found in these fishing grounds – birds, whales and people have been drawn to these rich waters for centuries.

# SEASCAPES

Many strange and wonderful rock formations can be seen on Djúpalónssandur beach. The largest formation is called Kerling, which juts out into the sea and is said to be a troll carrying a bundle of fish on her back. Closer to the camera is Steinnökkvi, which resembles the bow of a ship.

Ever since the settlement, Icelanders have dwelt near the coast, where the most wildlife is also concentrated. The Icelandic coastline is an ever changing and complex subject for photographers. Tides, beaches, surf, light and waves can completely transform the appearance of the cliffs and rocks along the shoreline in just a few hours. In terms of geological history, the coast has also undergone dramatic changes. Once there were beaches where today stand the bases of mountains. The lowlands by Landeyjasandur were once in the ocean and it is believed that in the late glacial period the landscape on the north side of Faxaflói bay was very different to how it is today. The Mýrar, Hnappadalur and Borgarfjörður districts are examples of landscapes which were once beneath the ocean. The careful observer can see that mountains now a long way inland were once magnificent coastal bird cliffs, some featuring ancient, wave-battered caves formed by coastal erosion. Iceland's coastline tells the story of the natural history of the land, as it varies across the country. The angle and layers of the land at the shore play a large part in how they are affected by coastal erosion.

For geology enthusiasts, the Icelandic coastline is a dream come true. Like a time machine, it transports the imagination on a journey through geological history and the formation of the land. The coast is also a dream come true for photographers. The churning ocean creates form and movement that provide a subject of unlimited interest. The coast is therefore one of the things that defines Iceland for photographers. It can also be a treacherous place, where danger may lurk behind every step and every wave, so it is vital to tread carefully. The ocean can sweep you away in an instant if you do not take care.

Stapi at Selvík, east of Þvottárskriður, is a rock that stands clear of the water at low tide but is overcome by the waves as the tide comes in.

North of Snartarstaðarnúpur lies Hvalvík. Stunning rock formations can be found along the beach, many of which are no less impressive than those at more popular destinations.

West of Stafsnes in the Westman Islands lie the Smáeyjar islands:
Hæna, Hani and Hrauney. The east side of Hæna, the most southerly of the three islands,
features the cave Kafhellir, which is so large that a small boat can sail inside.

Vestrahorn is a 454 m tall mountain on the peninsula between Skarðsfjörður and Papafjörður. This picturesque mountain looms up from the wet, sandy expanses of Stokksnes to the west. The landscape is extremely distinctive. There is a radar station on Stokksnes, which is managed by the Radar Agency of Iceland today but during the Cold War was an important piece of equipment operated by the U.S. Army.

The Reynisdrangar sea stacks rise 66 m out of the sea by Reynisfjall, a short distance from Vík í Mýrdal. Folklore has it that two trolls were dragging a three-sailed ship ashore when day broke and they were turned to stone.

Gatastapi is the name of a majestic rock formation a short distance from the shore at Hvalvík, north of Kópasker. The beach is home to a large number of rock formations and basalt columns.

Sunset in Skarðsvík on Öndverðarnes can be dazzling on a summer night as the sun grazes the horizon.

By Rauðinúpur, an ancient volcano on the Melrakkaslétta plain, stand two sea stacks. The western stack is called Sölvanöf and was once connected to the shore with a bridge that collapsed in 1962. The eastern stack is called Karlinn, home to a substantial gannet colony. Puffins, guillemots, fulmars and other species also nest on both stacks.

Svalþúfa is a tuff promontory believed to be part of an old volcano. From Svalþúfa there is a spectacular view over the Lóndrangar stacks and a bird cliff called Þúfubjarg. It is said that the Devil and Kolbeinn Grímsson once had a poetry contest on the cliff edge. Kolbeinn won by inventing a new metre, which was named after him.

Hvítserkur is a 15-m-high sea stack on the western shore of Húnafjörður. Down on the beach it is possible to walk right up to the stack.

Arnarstapi on Snæfellsnes peninsula is a famous site from the Icelandic sagas, featuring in the saga of Bárður Snæfellsás. The area is characterised by large numbers of birds, strange rock formations along the shore and the proximity to Snæfellsjökull glacier.

The Kálfafellstindar mountains tower majestically over the site of the former church at Kálfafellsstaður. It is the birthplace of Torfhildur Þorsteinsdóttir (1845–1918), the first Icelandic author to write historical fiction and the first Icelandic woman to make a living from writing.

Gatklettur is a distinctive cliff by Arnarstapi on Snæfellsnes peninsula.
It is the remains of an old dike eroded by the sea into a stunning formation.
Birds nest on the cliff despite the turbulent waves and significant tidal range.

Gatastakkur is one of a great number of rock formations along the coastline at Rauðanes in Þistilsfjörður. Further to the north lies Stakkar, its spectacular form also created by the sea over the years.

The island of Grímsey is 5.3 $km^2$ and lies 41 km north of the main coast of Iceland. The Arctic circle cuts through the island, which is truly a natural paradise, despite the fact that the environment can be harsh and unforgiving. Around 60 species of birds frequent the island and over a 100 varieties of plant can be found.

# THE WINTER

Horses were brought to Iceland by Norse settlers over 1,000 years ago. The Icelandic horse is a breed related to the Norwegian Lyngshest and has Mongolian origins. It is not a large breed compared to many others, but it is exceptionally strong, tough and incredibly hardy.

"When there are two fine-weather mornings in succession in Iceland, it is as if all the cares of life have vanished for good" – so it says in the novel *World Light* by the Nobel Prize-winning Icelandic author Halldór Laxness. It is hard to find a better description of the national character. Icelanders are quick to forget catastrophe with the arrival of fine weather.

You can soon find your life in danger if you fail to respect the weather. The Icelandic search and rescue services are kept busy all year round, not least when people set off on trips in spite of a bad weather forecast.

The coldest months are December and January, when the average temperature is around 0–10°C. Iceland has a temperate climate, with the temperature significantly affected by the Gulf Stream. If there is no landfast sea ice, it is warmer along the coast than further inland. The average temperature in the warmest months of the year is only 10°C. It is often said that if you don't like the weather in Iceland, wait five minutes. It can change in an instant.

Harsh winter weather has made a deep impression on the national character. Loss of life due to bad weather is most common at sea and in avalanches. On 8 March 1700 a deadly storm hit at sea, during which 140 people drowned and many boats were sunk. That morning the weather had been fine, but it suddenly turned with a southerly gale. In a storm on 9 March 1658, 132 sailors from the Westman Islands and Stafsnes were drowned. On 26 October 1995, an avalanche hit Flateyri after a violent storm had raged in the West Fjords for several days. Twenty people were killed in the avalanche. These events are just a small sample of the history that has wormed its way into the national consciousness.

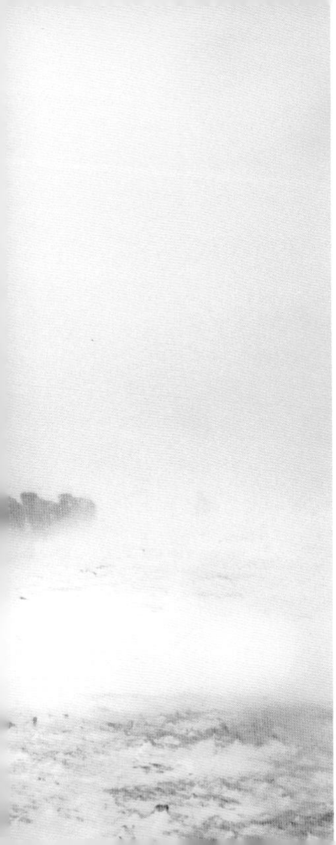

Throughout the ages, the Icelandic horse has weathered storms and gales and is well adapted to the Icelandic climate and landscape. It is not a demanding breed with regards to food or accommodation. In the worst storms, however, it will seek shelter.

The Icelandic horse is a versatile breed, distinguished by its five gaits. There are around 70,000–80,000 horses in Iceland and they often live to over 25 years old. Horses are herd animals and seek the companionship of other horses.

A winter storm by the Kálfatindar mountains in Hornstrandir shows the toughness and resilience of the people who once managed to make their homes in this remote location. Over the summer months the bird cliffs teem with life, but in the winter the Arctic fox must eke out a living in a harsh environment.

The territory of the Arctic fox is defined by drifting snow, frost and fire. It is believed that the Arctic fox came to Iceland around 10,000 years ago, at the end of the last ice age. It was therefore the only native land mammal in Iceland at the time of the settlement and over the centuries has adapted to the variable climate and limited availability of food.

The basalt formation near Borgir in Grímsey is exceptionally beautiful. In the old days people covered the columns with tablecloths and served coffee on them in fine weather and other celebrations. Borgarhöfðinn, Hellugjögurinn and Emelíuklappirnar, here lapped by the freezing winter tide, are a continuous formation of basalt columns on the southern side of the island.

Puffins spend the winter months at sea, but towards the end of April or beginning of May, they begin to think of nesting. A puffin in the snow is rather an unusual sight, but this one was spotted in late May on Grímsey, waiting impatiently for the summer.

Around 30% of the Icelandic Arctic fox population is white, but brown is much more common. The Arctic fox has survived here since the last glacial period. Since the settlement, foxes have been persecuted by humans and still are today. Around 6,000 adults and cubs are hunted each year, a figure that has never been higher. Iceland is the only country in Europe, and probably in the entire Western world, that allows the killing of adults and cubs in the breeding season, evidence of the deep-rooted hatred of the fox as a pest in farming communities. The authorities pay hunters to kill foxes and mink.

Grímsey is the most northerly inhabited island in Iceland. There are few places where the contrast between summer and winter is so stark. Over the winter months, cold winds from the Atlantic ocean howl over the island, which is enveloped in darkness. As the sun rises higher in the sky, the island comes to life and is soon teeming with birds.

HIÐ ÍSLENZKA REÐASAFN • THE ICELANDIC PHALLOLOGICAL MUSEUM •

26 OKT. 2013

**Admission for 1 person**

**1.700 Kr.**

---

**The Icelandic Phallological Museum**

**Laugavegi 116, Reykjavik.**

**Tel: +354-5616663**

**www.phallus.is /**

**phallus@phallus.is** Nr: 23192

**Snaps ehf**
Þórsgötu 1
101 Reykjavík
Kt.: 4112110880, VSK nr.: 110000

---

Reikn. prentaður: 26.10.2018 21:42:57
Sölumaður: Snæfríður
Kassi nr.: 1
Bar 29B

*** Staðgreitt ***

| Fl: Lýsing: | Verð: |
|---|---|
| U3 Klassísk klúbbsamloka | 2.890kr |
| **Samtals:** | **2.890kr** |
| U3 VSK: 11,00% af 2.890kr | 286kr |

Takk fyrir komuna !

Þessi reikningur á uppruna [illegible]
bókhaldskerfi skv. reglugerð nr. 505/20[illegible]

Hornvík is the heart of Hornstrandir. It would be hard to find a lonelier and more remote spot in Iceland. There is no phone signal and it is a long sea journey to the nearest inhabited area. Polar bears are not uncommon visitors to Iceland, having come ashore around 250 times since the settlement.

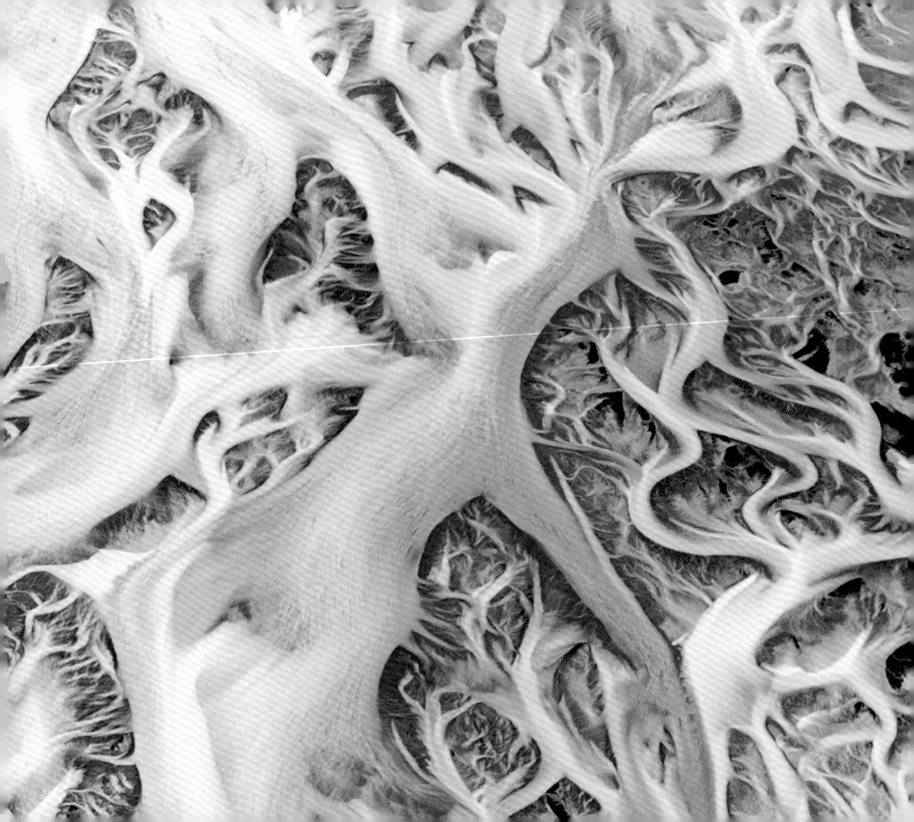

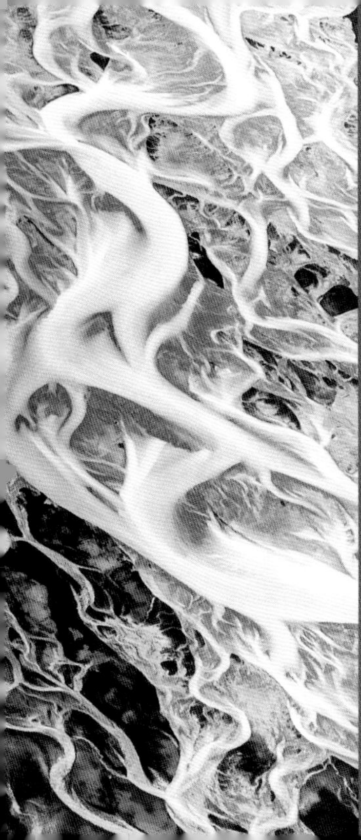

# ABSTRACTS

Tungnaá river winds its way through the sandy plains a short distance from Snjóöldufjallgarður in the Fjallabak Nature Reserve. From the air the milky glacial water resembles nothing more than a web of capillaries.

Iceland is a paradise for landscape photographers. The light, the glaciers, the volcanic activity and the highlands are spectacular subjects. We are used to viewing the world through our own eyes, with our feet planted firmly on the ground. Looking at the landscape through a bird's-eye view opens up a new world. Rivers, streams, lakes and glaciers form breathtaking abstract patterns when seen from the air. Water flowing through black sands in certain conditions also forms the most peculiar patterns, making it hard to tell whether a picture was taken from the air or the ground. It is easy to see abstract patterns in the colours and lines of a river. They can be enchanting and are distinctive features of both the highlands and the glacial rivers winding their way to the sea.

As seen from the air, the milky glacial water flowing through the rivers Markarfljót or Tungnaá resembles a web of coronary arteries. Life-giving arteries transporting nutrients and outwash deposits around the country. A bird's-eye view is not the only way to reveal the abstract forms of the land. It is easy to get carried away by your own imagination, spotting various patterns in the cliffs and rocks. We see what we want to see. Faces, trolls and enigmatic images appear if we give our imaginations free reign. The creator of the images is nature itself, as we simply look on in wonder. This is one of the distinctive features of Iceland. Throughout the ages, it has been easy to spot monsters and ghosts in the dark and the fog, as evident in Icelandic folklore. Unconventional perspectives bring us closer to that world. We see monsters, trolls and strange figures etched into the land itself. All conjured by our own imaginations.

Hellnar, just west of Arnarstapi, was one of the largest fishing villages on the Snæfellsnes peninsula. The sea has created many strange and beautiful rock formations in the area and the birdlife is extremely diverse.

The Markarfljót river has its source in Mýrdalsjökull glacier, and to a certain extent Eyjafjallajökull. The river has flooded plains and flatlands and frequently causes significant damage to farming land on its way to the sea. Ancient eyewitness accounts claim that monsters have been spotted in Markarfljót.

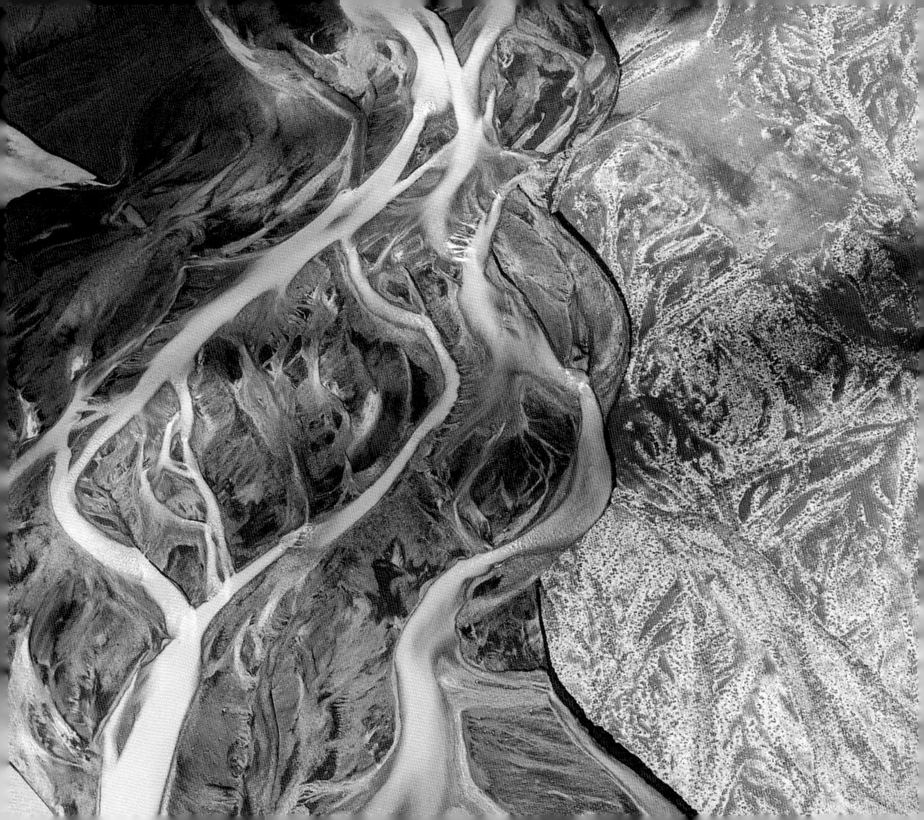

The milky Tungnaá river meets the flatlands near the Kattahryggir trail. The river has its source by the Kerlingar mountains on the western edge of Vatnajökull glacier and can become extremely powerful. Travellers in the highlands have often found it a formidable obstacle.

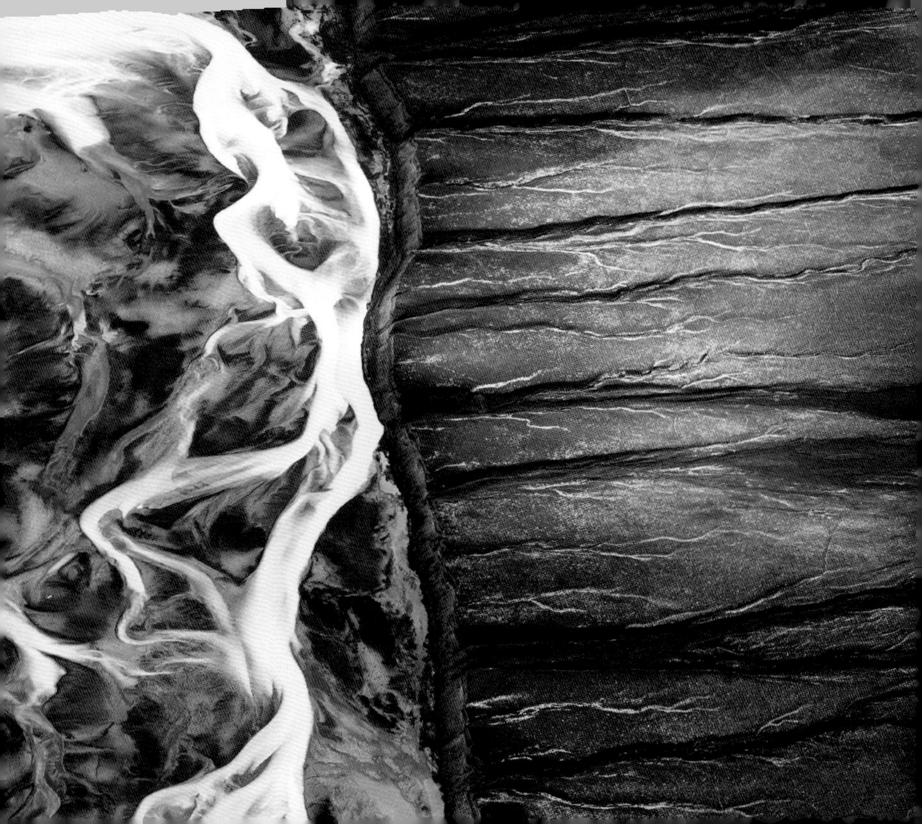

Rounded grooves can be seen in the seaweed-covered bedrock at Flæðivík by the Lóndrangar sea stacks. Over the years, the tide has created spectacular patterns in the rock. Pebbles that become lodged in the grooves accelerate the coastal erosion.

"The water drop hollows the stone", according to the Icelandic proverb. At Lóndrangar on Snæfellsnes peninsula, coastal erosion has formed basins in the hard rock.

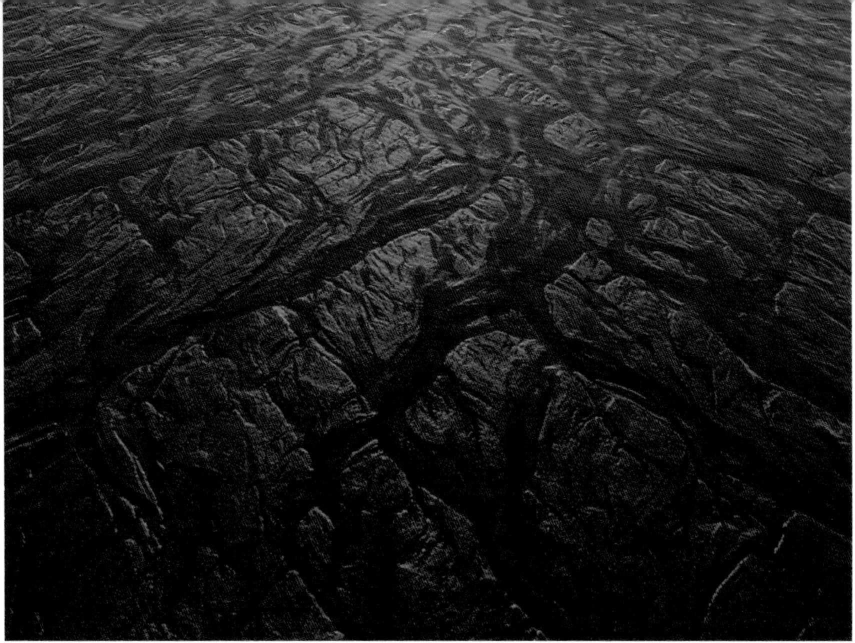

These crevasses in Fjallsjökull glacier show beyond all doubt how treacherous glaciers can be. Fjallsjökull is an outlet glacier, part of Öræfajökull.

The blazing red of the evening sun shows patterns in the sand at Skarðsvíkurfjara beach at Öndverðarnes.

# Acknowledgements

Einar and Gyða have pursued photography seriously since 2005. They are both among the most renowned nature and landscape photographers in Iceland. From the very start they have specialised in bird, animal and landscape photography. People and human constructions do not feature strongly, with the focus kept on nature in its various forms. They have participated in a diverse range of photography projects and their work has been displayed extensively in Iceland and abroad. They spend weeks at a time travelling around Iceland with their cameras and strive to raise awareness of the importance of protecting untouched nature.

This book is the product of ten years of photography. We have met many people on our travels through Iceland and it would be impossible to thank everyone who did us a favour. We must, however, mention Brynjar Ágústsson and Steinunn Inga Óttarsdóttir, as well as Völundur Jónsson and Helga Kvam, who we are lucky enough to call our friends and travel companions. Their knowledge of Iceland and of the art of photography has been invaluable for us, and they are an endless fount of wisdom.

The photographer Daníel Bergmann, the mammalian ecologist Ester Rut Unnsteinsdóttir, the ecologist Ólafur K. Níelsen, the animal ecologist Kristinn H. Skarphéðinsson and the biologist Róbert Arnar Stefánsson have also been an invaluable source of help for us, as well as the staffs of the Icelandic Institute of Natural History and the Environment Agency of Iceland, who have assisted us in various ways and given us permission to photograph protected species.

The hospitable people of Grímsey, our families, brave pilots and the staff at Forlagið also spring to mind when we think of all those to whom we owe a debt of gratitude. Without the help of those above and countless others who have encouraged and inspired us, this book would never have been.

*Einar Guðmann and Gyða Henningsdóttir*

www.gudmann.is www.gyda.is

# Bibliography


Ari Trausti Guðmundsson and Pétur Þorleifsson 2004, *Íslensk fjöll*. Mál og menning. Reykjavík.
Björn Hróarsson and Sigurður Sveinn Jónsson 1991, *Hverir á Íslandi*. Mál og menning. Reykjavík.
Daníel Bergmann 2004. *Skaftafell National Park*. JPV Publishers. Reykjavík.
Ester Rut Unnsteinsdóttir 2016. Refastofninn. *Veiðidagbók 2016*. The Environment Agency of Iceland. Akurey
Guðmundur Páll Ólafsson 1990, *Perlur í náttúru Íslands*. Mál og menning. Reykjavík.
Guðmundur Páll Ólafsson 1995, *Ströndin í náttúru Íslands*. Mál og menning. Reykjavík.
Guðmundur Páll Ólafsson 2006, *Fuglar í náttúru Íslands*. Mál og menning. Reykjavík.
Guðmundur Páll Ólafsson 2013, *Vatnið í náttúru Íslands*. Mál og menning. Reykjavík.
Helgi Daníelsson (ed.) 2003, *Grímsey og Grímseyingar*. Akrafjallsútgáfan. Akranes.
Jón Kr. Gunnarsson 1992, *Íslenskir fossar. Skuggsjá*. Hafnarförður.
Kristinn Haukur Skarphéðinsson 2013, *Haförninn*. BirdLife Iceland. Reykjavík.
Páll Ásgeir Ásgeirsson 2007. *Hornstrandir*. Mál og menning. Reykjavík.
Páll Hersteinsson (ed.) and Jón Baldur Hlíðberg (illus.) 2005. *Íslensk spendýr*. Vaka-Helgafell, Reykjavík.
Páll Hersteinsson 2006. Report written for the Icelandic Institute of Natural History. *Íslenski villiminkurinn – staða þekkingar*. University of Iceland Institute of Biology. Reykjavík.
Páll Hersteinsson 2006. Íslenski tófustofninn. *Veiðidagbók 2006*. The Environment Agency of Iceland. Akureyri
Páll Hersteinsson and Guttormur Sigbjarnarson (eds.) 1993. *Villt íslensk spendýr*. The Icelandic Natural History Society and the Icelandic Environment Association. Reykjavík.
Sigurður Ægisson and Jón Baldur Hlíðberg (illus.) 1996, *Ísfygla*: Íslenskir fuglar. Sigurður Ægisson. Grenjaðarstað.
Steinar Rafn Beck 2016. Refa- og minkaveiðar sveitarfélaga. *Veiðidagbók 2016*. The Environment Agency of Iceland. Akureyri.
Steindór Steindórsson and Þorsteinn Jósepsson 1981. *Landið þitt Ísland*. Reykjavík.
Ævar Petersen, Jón Baldur Hlíðberg 1998. Stofnstærð. *Íslenskir fuglar*. Vaka-Helgafell, Reykjavík.

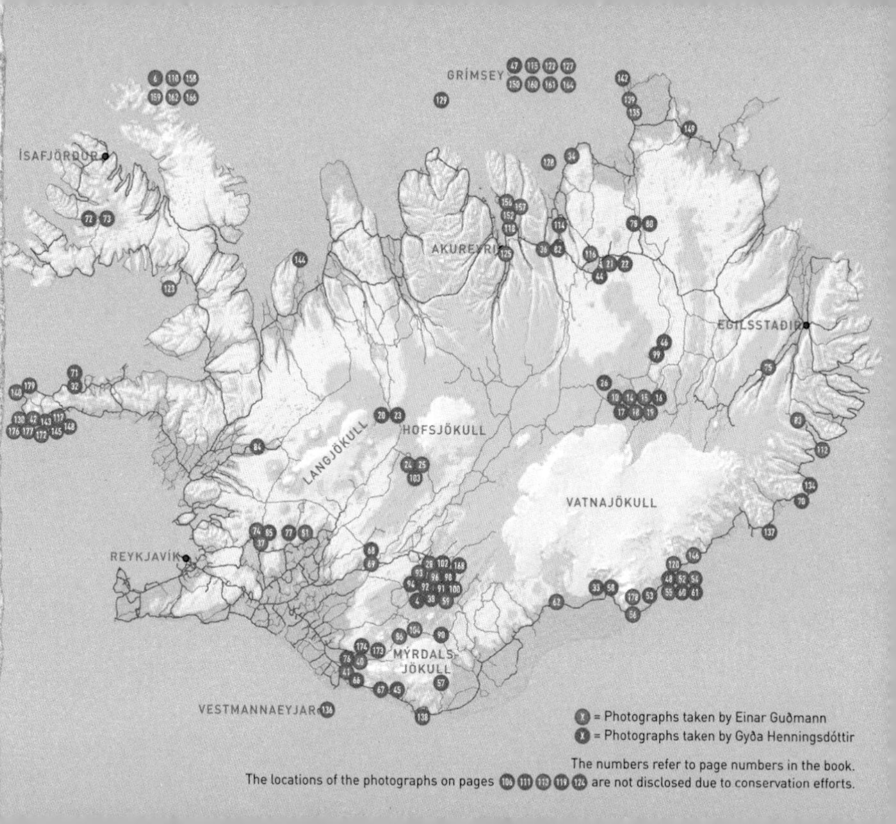
GRÍMSEY
ÍSAFJÖRÐUR
AKUREYRI
EGILSSTAÐIR
HOFSJÖKULL
LANGJÖKULL
VATNAJÖKULL
REYKJAVÍK
MÝRDALS-
JÖKULL
VESTMANNAEYJAR
= Photographs taken by Einar Guðmann
= Photographs taken by Gyða Henningsdóttir
The numbers refer to page numbers in the book.
The locations of the photographs on pages 106 111 113 119 124 are not disclosed due to conservation efforts.